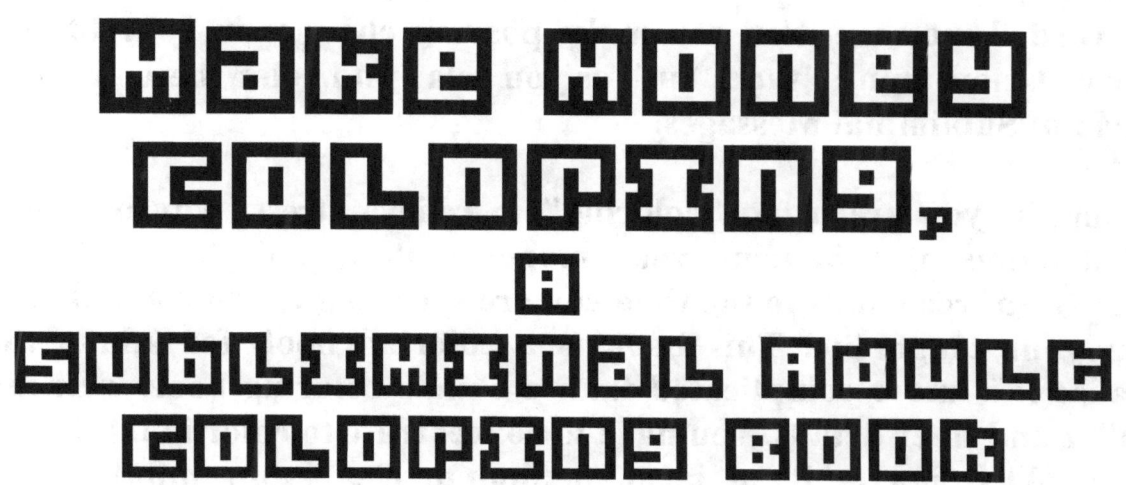

Make Money Coloring, A Subliminal Adult Coloring Book

volume 1

by
Stephen Jorgensen

published by
CyberSuccess Publishing
Honolulu, Hawaii

This Adult coloring book has interesting word shape and verbal subliminal designs for you to color. But in the process of coloring, your subconscious mind absorbs the subliminal messages they present and this can help you change your attitude, feelings and behavior related to the worded message. You can make positive changes in your life when your conscious mind "tunes out" as you relax and color these pages. It is a form of Subliminal Messages.

As long as you are using "coloring" to relieve stress, why not get the added bonus of enhancing your money making abilities at the same time? It's a free bonus to the time you are spending to relax and de-stress from your tough life. This book is a coloring book for adults that's because it is more complicated than a child's coloring book with much smaller and finer details. You have to concentrate to color in all the small shapes. That makes it an ideal method to clear your mind of many negative thoughts and it helps you relieve stress. Coloring will reduce anxiety, and help you focus and will bring you more mindfulness. It is therapeutic.

And because you are focusing on coloring the shapes going mainly by feeling, not by thinking, your conscious mind sort of shuts down, this not only relieves stress, (of the conscious mind judging your every thought and action), but it opens your subconscious mind to barely perceived information you normally wouldn't have noticed. In general, the conscious mind acts as a gatekeeper, choosing which "facts" it encounters are important to you and should be saved or acted upon, and which "facts" are not important, or are not relevant due to the "fact" that they are "false".

The subconscious mind, on the other hand, acts more like a computer that takes whatever information it is programmed with and uses that information as "facts" to influence you with vague feelings that you should do such and such. Subliminal messages are messages that are below the level of conscious perception. You are not consciously aware of them. But the subconscious mind can be aware of them, and can act on them. The subconscious mind can handle much more information than the conscious mind. If you are concentrating on reading a book for example, the conscious mind is focused on that, but is unaware of the TV, of surrounding conversations, of room temperature, of your heart rate, of the pain in your hip,etc. All these sort of things that the subconscious mind is keeping track of, the "conscious" you doesn't notice.

So in our lives, too many times we have been told, sometimes verbally, sometimes just by a negative glance, that we can't succeed at something, that we are no good at something and the conscious mind looks at that "fact" and compares it with past actions, and sees, yes we did fail at that previously, and it decides that is "true". From then on it tends to reject new information that perhaps we are not so bad, that perhaps we could succeed in that area, and the conscious mind ignores that new "factoid" and doesn't save it in the memory because it isn't a relevant fact. If we could just bypass the conscious mind sometimes and reprogram our brains, we could move towards greater success in our lives. That's what subliminal messages do, they bypass the gatekeeper conscious mind, and build new information in the subconscious mind, information that could lead to a positive change in our lives. Technically, since all the messages presented in these coloring pages are visible to your conscious mind if you focus on them, they are not subliminal, (below the level of perception) but would be called supraliminal, (above the absolute level of perception). But if you can turn off the conscious mind by coloring, the messages can seep into the unconscious mind with positive effects. Scientists have found such supraliminal messages can effect a measurable change as long as it is simple, and the person has a desire to change. It's not much, at most 10% but it is something, and everything helps.

These designs are for colorists that would like to use their coloring time to change their lives in a positive direction. The artist has done other coloring books but he specializes in bigger Hawaiian paintings. All the works included here are refined by the Hawaiian artist Stephen E Jorgensen. He has over 200 other works of beautiful Hawaiian art available on his Etsy website. Most of his work is large canvas wall hangings, some of which are reduced to coloring pages for his Relaxing Hawaiian Scenes Coloring books. See these artworks at hawaiiseascapes.etsy.com.

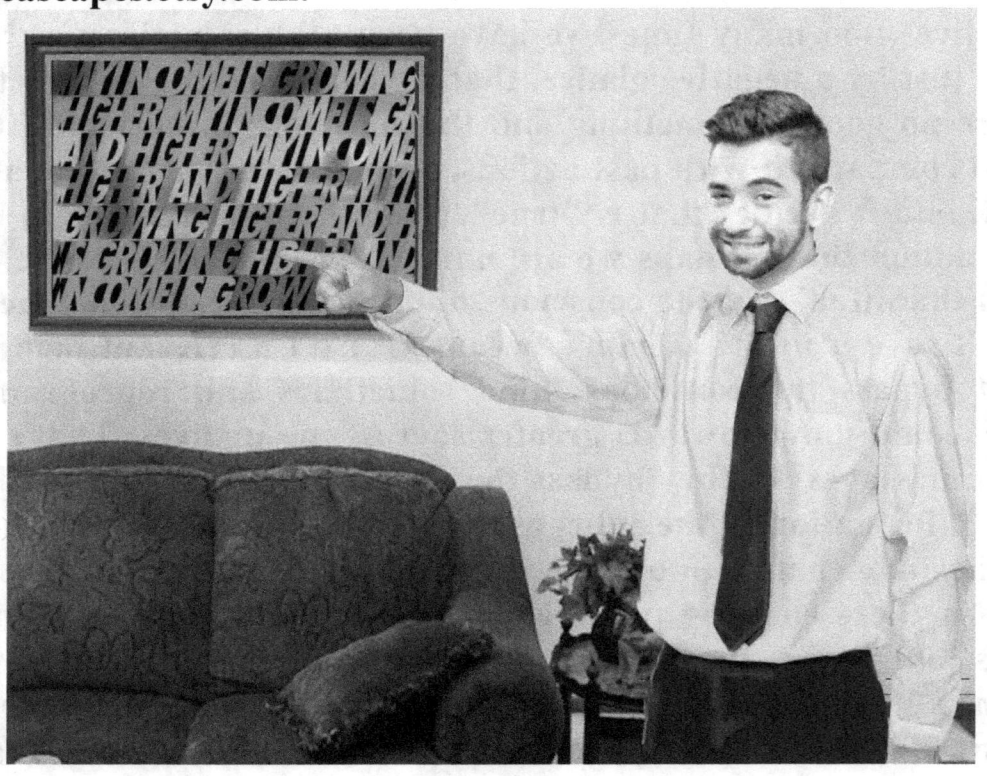

Feel free to make copies of the pages you are working on so you can try different coloring schemes. If you develop one that you really like, you can order a large poster sized coloring pages from our web site at Etsy. hawaiiseascapes.etsy.com and then make your own poster art. They come in 11" X 17" and 17" X 22" and 24" X 36" sizes.

Make Money Coloring, A Subliminal Adult Coloring Book

ISBN-13:
978-1548241247

ISBN-10:
1548241245

THE

mere words

are fun

TO COLOR

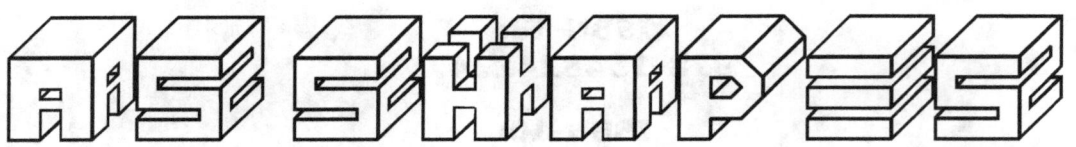

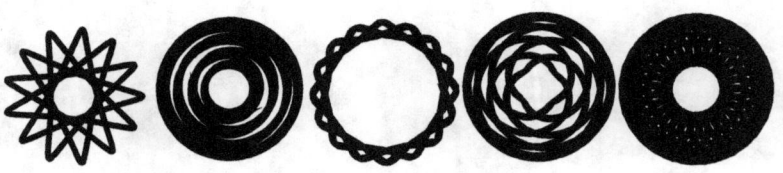

Make Money Coloring, A Subliminal Adult Coloring Book

These designs are for colorists that want to use coloring to positively influence their lives. This artist has done other coloring books and is now doing a whole series of Subliminal coloring books, check out some of the series, Make Money, Lose Weight, Attract Love, Control Anger, and Achieve Success. A helpful series, but for his art, he specializes in bigger Hawaiian paintings. All the works included here are by the Hawaiian artist Stephen E Jorgensen. He has over 200 other works of beautiful Hawaiian art available on his Etsy website. Most of his work is large canvas wall hangings, some of which are reduced to coloring pages for his Relaxing Hawaiian Scenes Coloring books. See these artworks at hawaiiseascapes.etsy.com.

Some of my other coloring books show the colored-in versions in full color on the covers of their books, but with the designs here of just words and letter shapes, it doesn't matter at all how they are colored, so they are not all depicted on the covers. Of course you are free to chose your own colors. As such they are a delight to color. Just go by what you feel, let the thinking mind turn off. Enjoy coloring, and let the subliminal messages push you towards the success you desire!

This Subliminal Coloring Therapy
will relax you. It is fun.

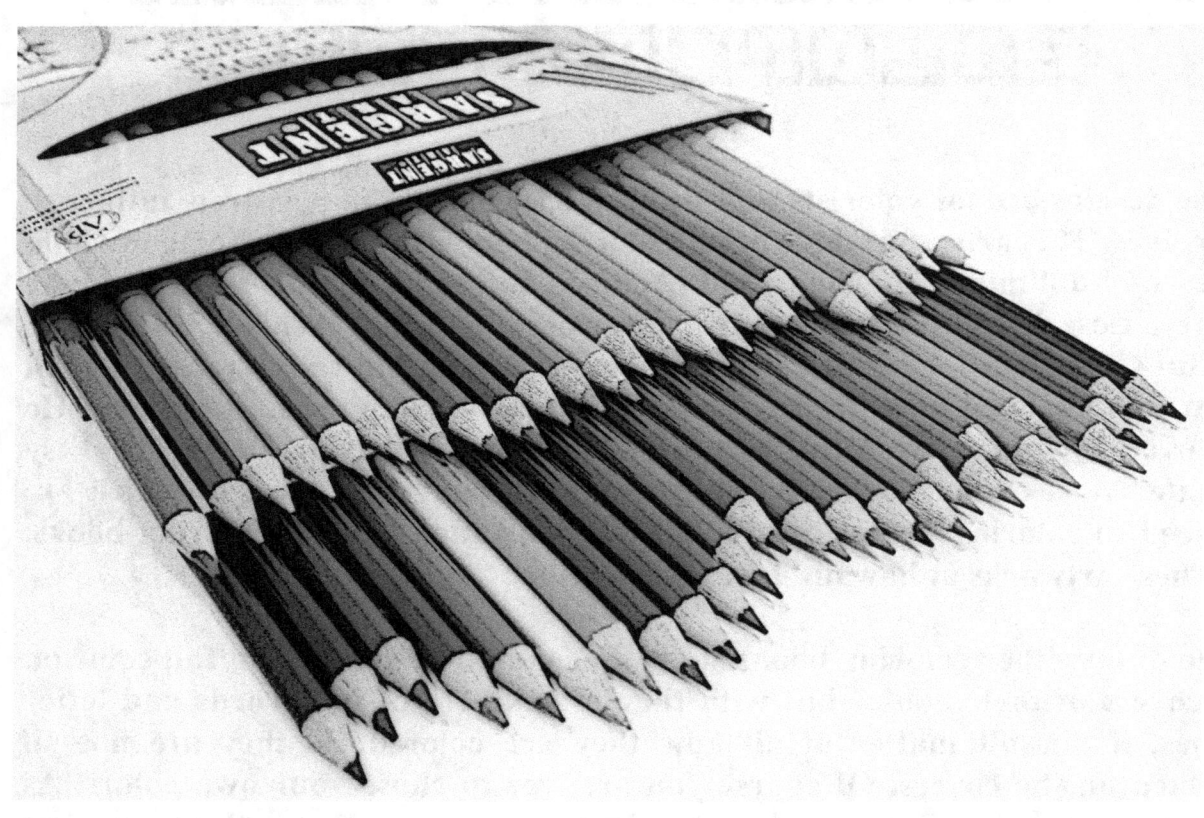

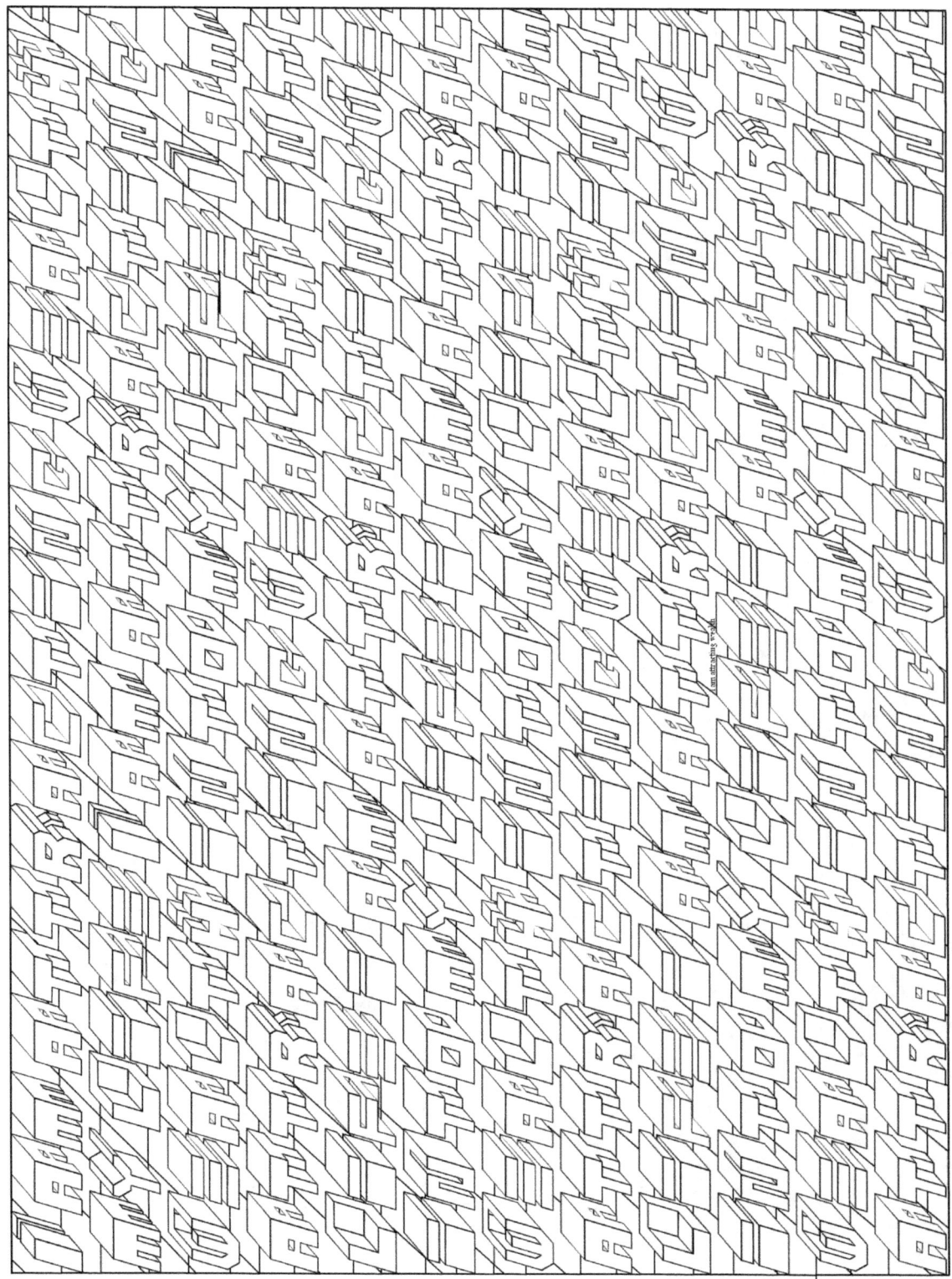

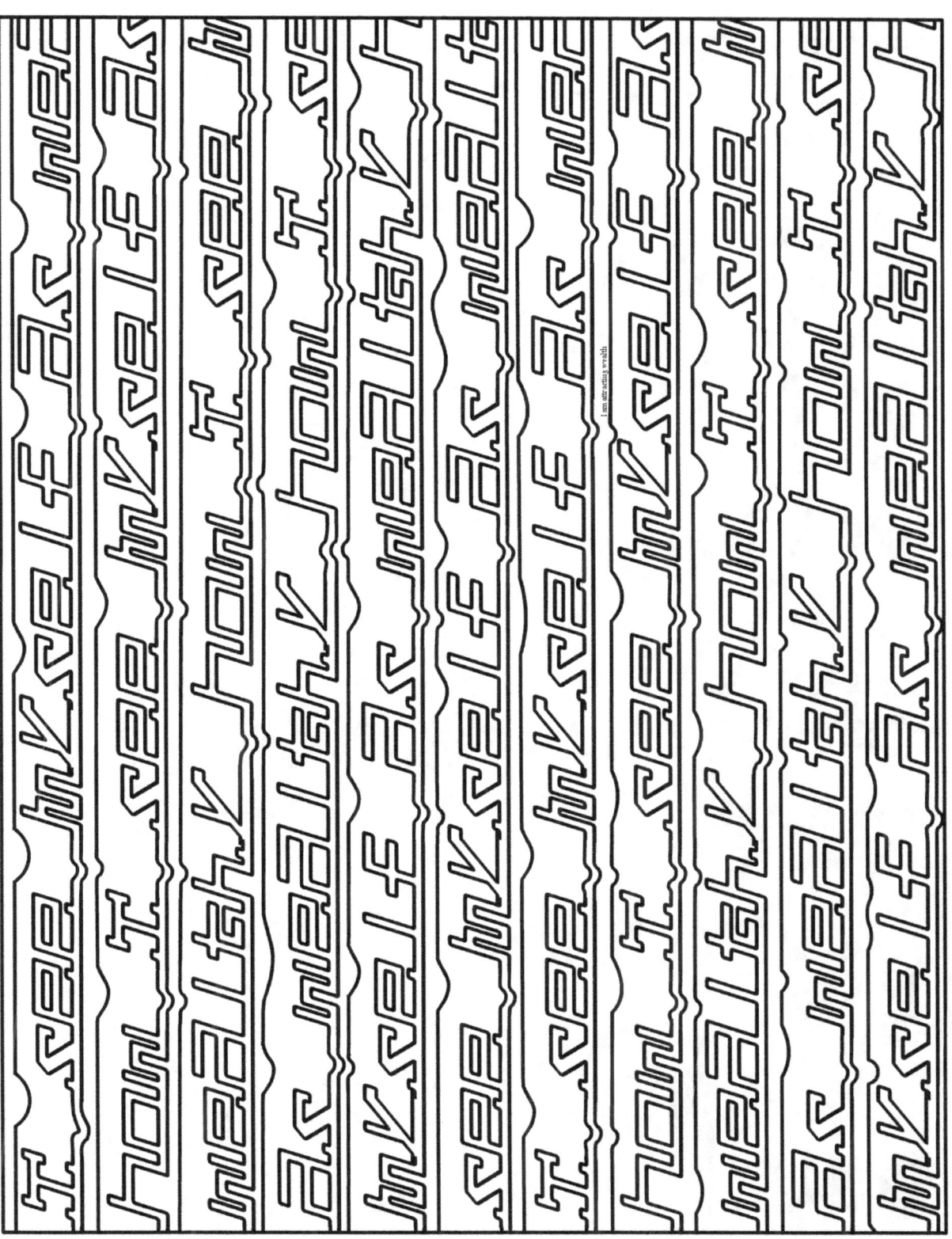

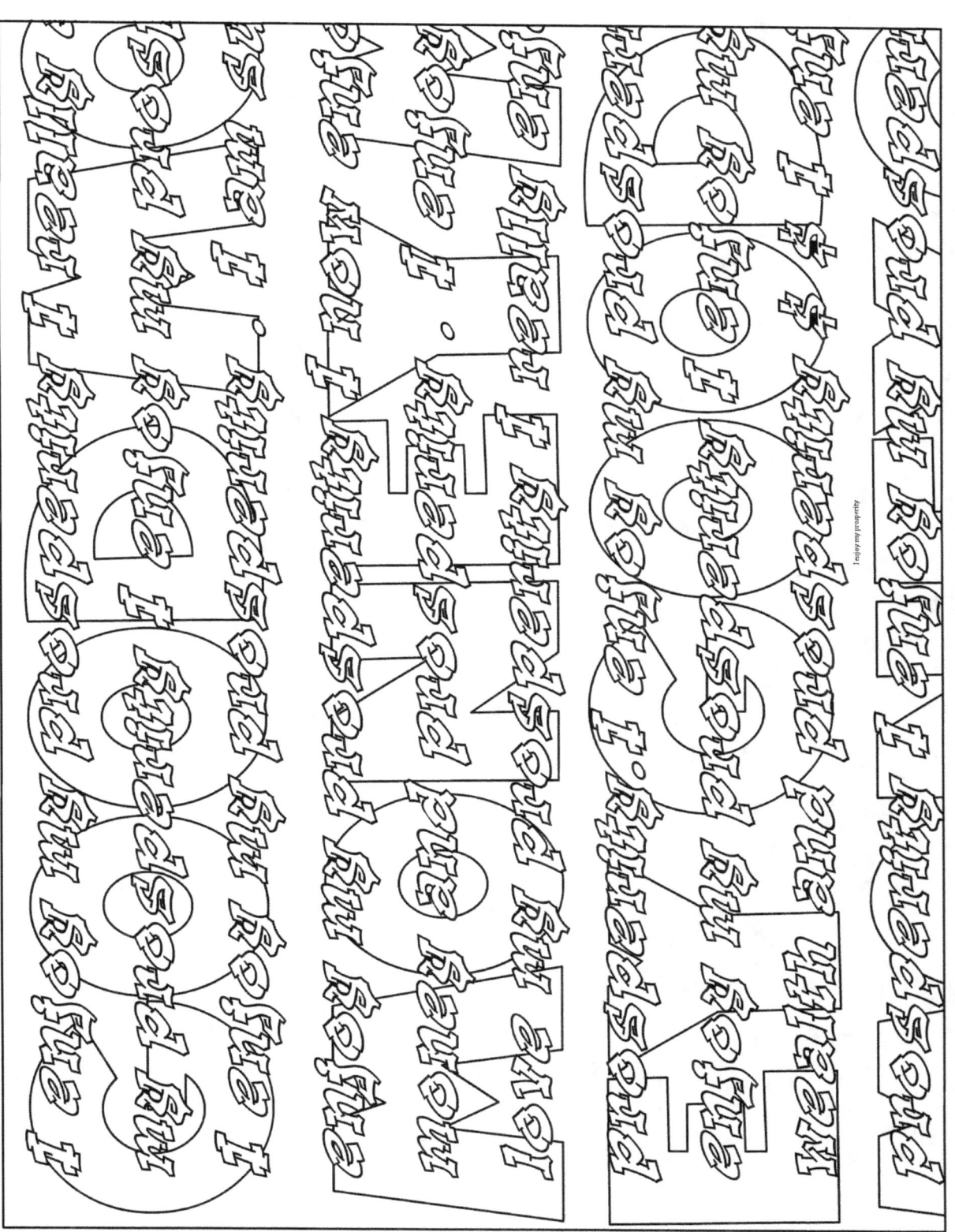

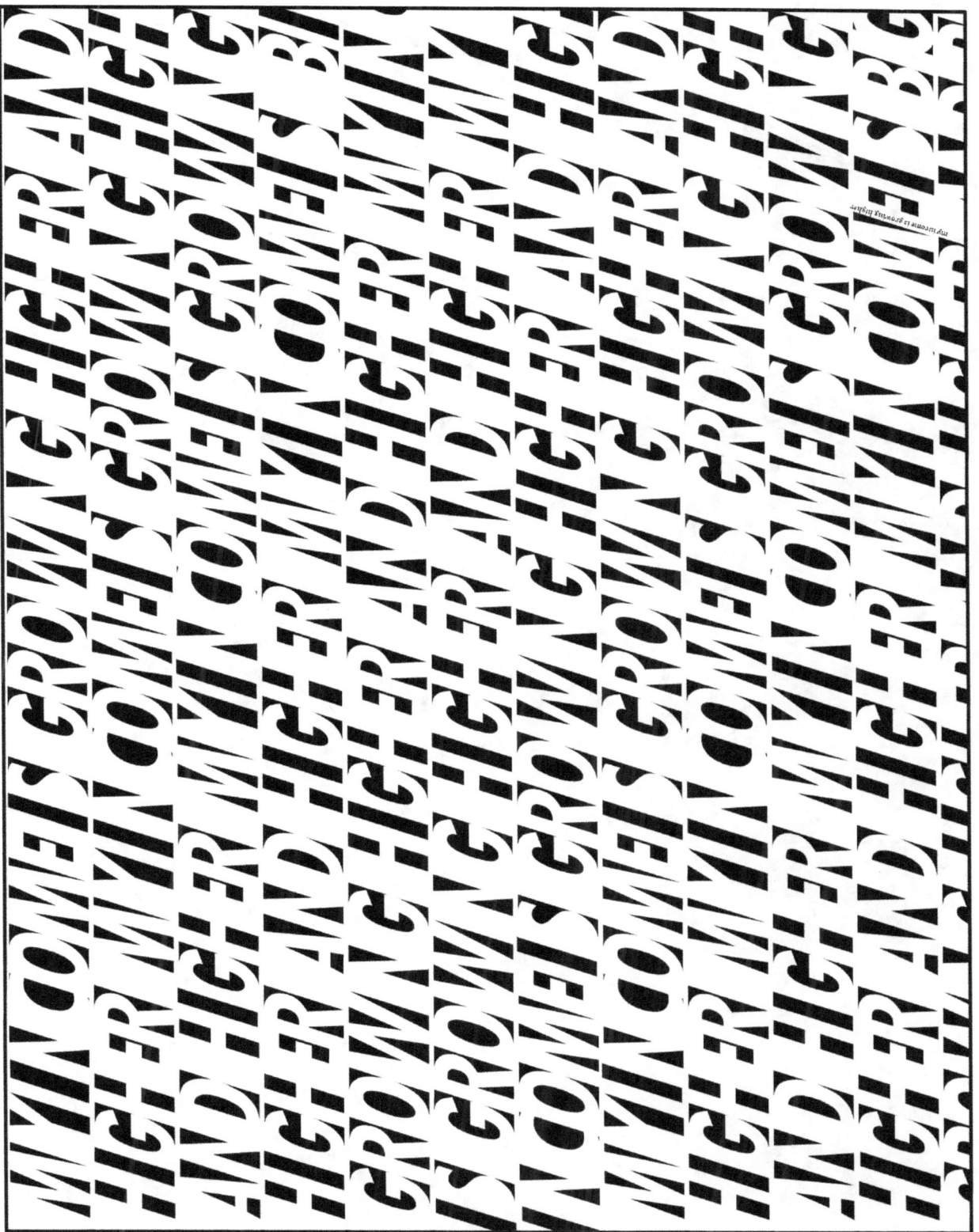

my income is growing higher.

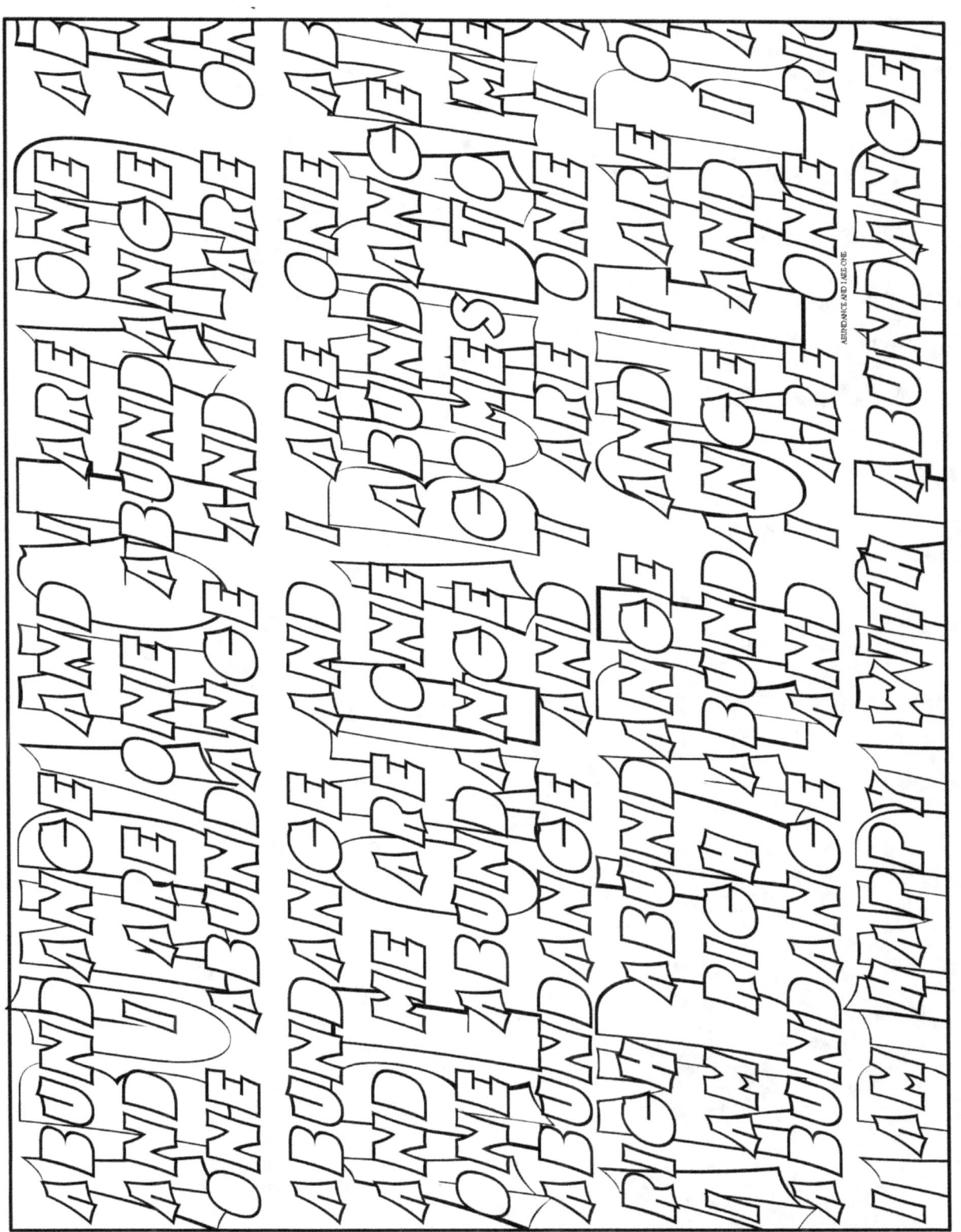

Money is being attracted to me

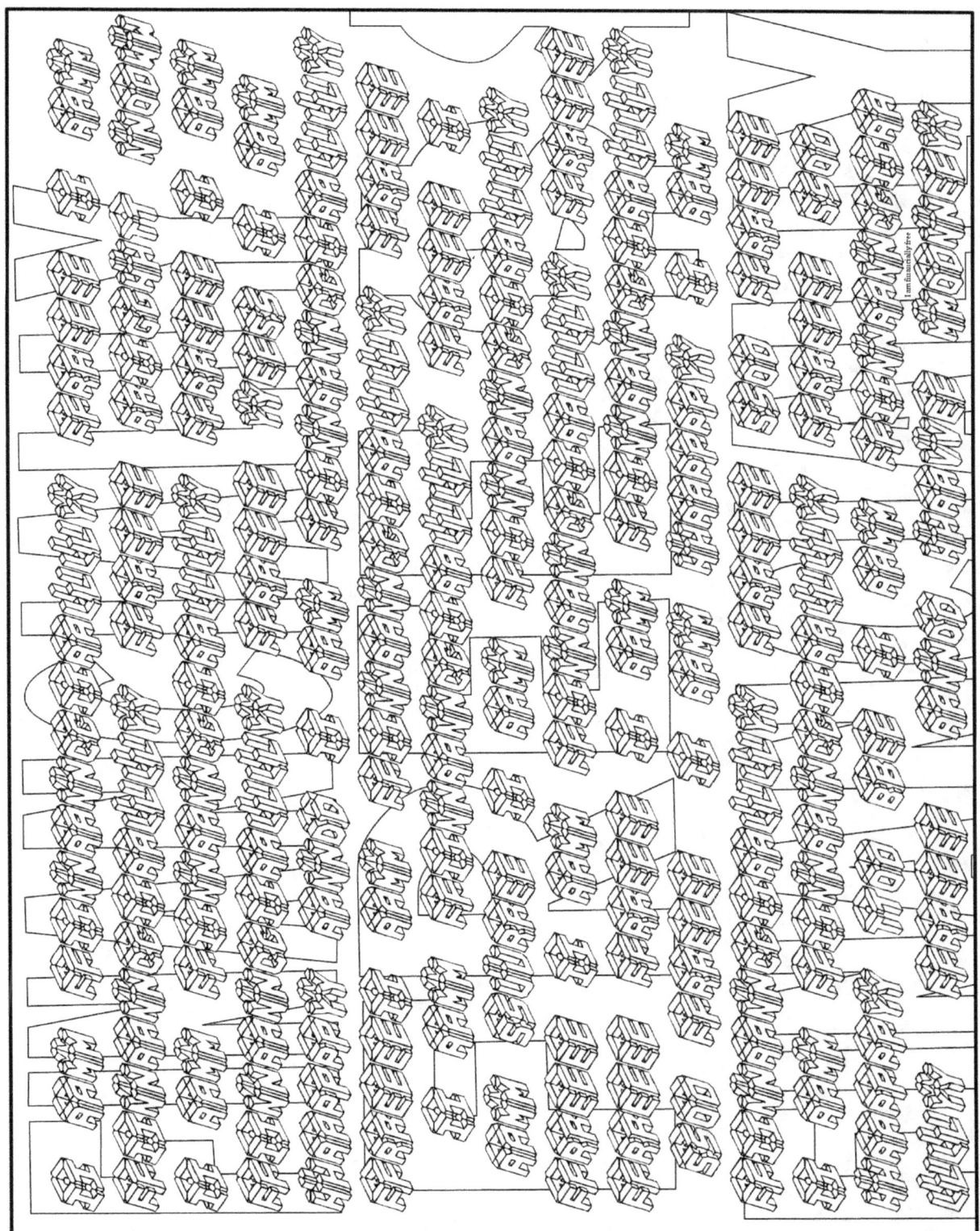

I am financially free

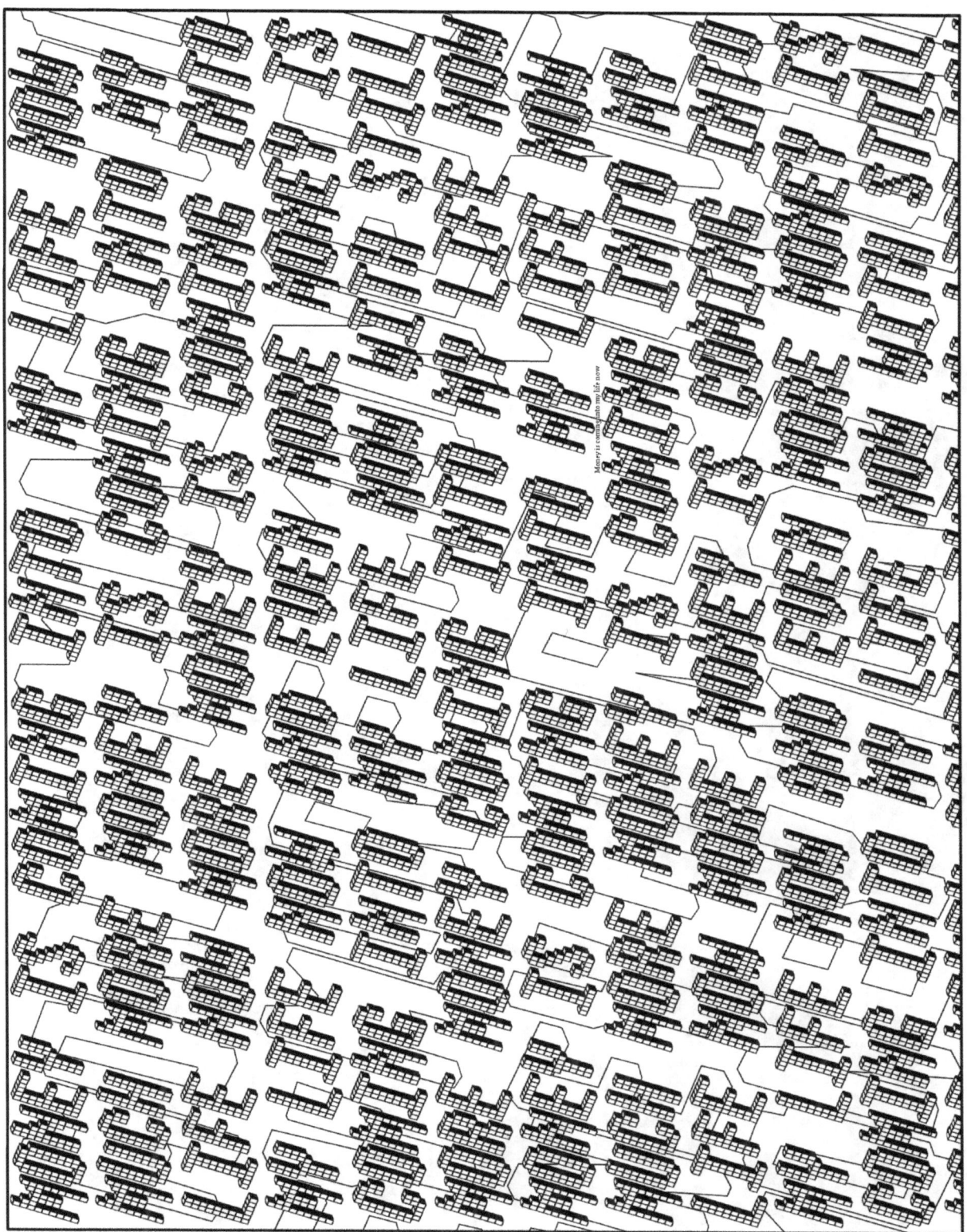

Money is coming into my life now

MY DESIRE IS TO BRING MONEY IN ABUNDANCE INTO MY LIFE AND I WILL SUCCEED MY DESIRE IS TO BRING MONEY IN ABUNDANCE INTO MY LIFE AND I WILL SUCCEED IN MY DESIRE IS TO BRING MONEY IN ABUNDANCE INTO MY LIFE AND I WILL SUCCEED MY DESIRE IS TO BRING MONEY IN ABUNDANCE INTO MY LIFE AND I WILL SUCCEED IN MY DESIRE IS TO BRING MONEY IN ABUNDANCE INTO MY LIFE AND I WILL SUCCEED MY DESIRE IS TO BRING MONEY IN ABUNDANCE INTO MY LIFE AND I WILL SUCCEED IN MY DESIRE IS TO BRING MONEY INTO MY DESIRE IS TO BRING MONEY INTO MY LIFE AND I WILL SUCCEED IN MY DESIRE IS TO BRING MONEY INTO MY DESIRE IS TO BRING MONEY INTO

My desire is bring money and abundance into my life.

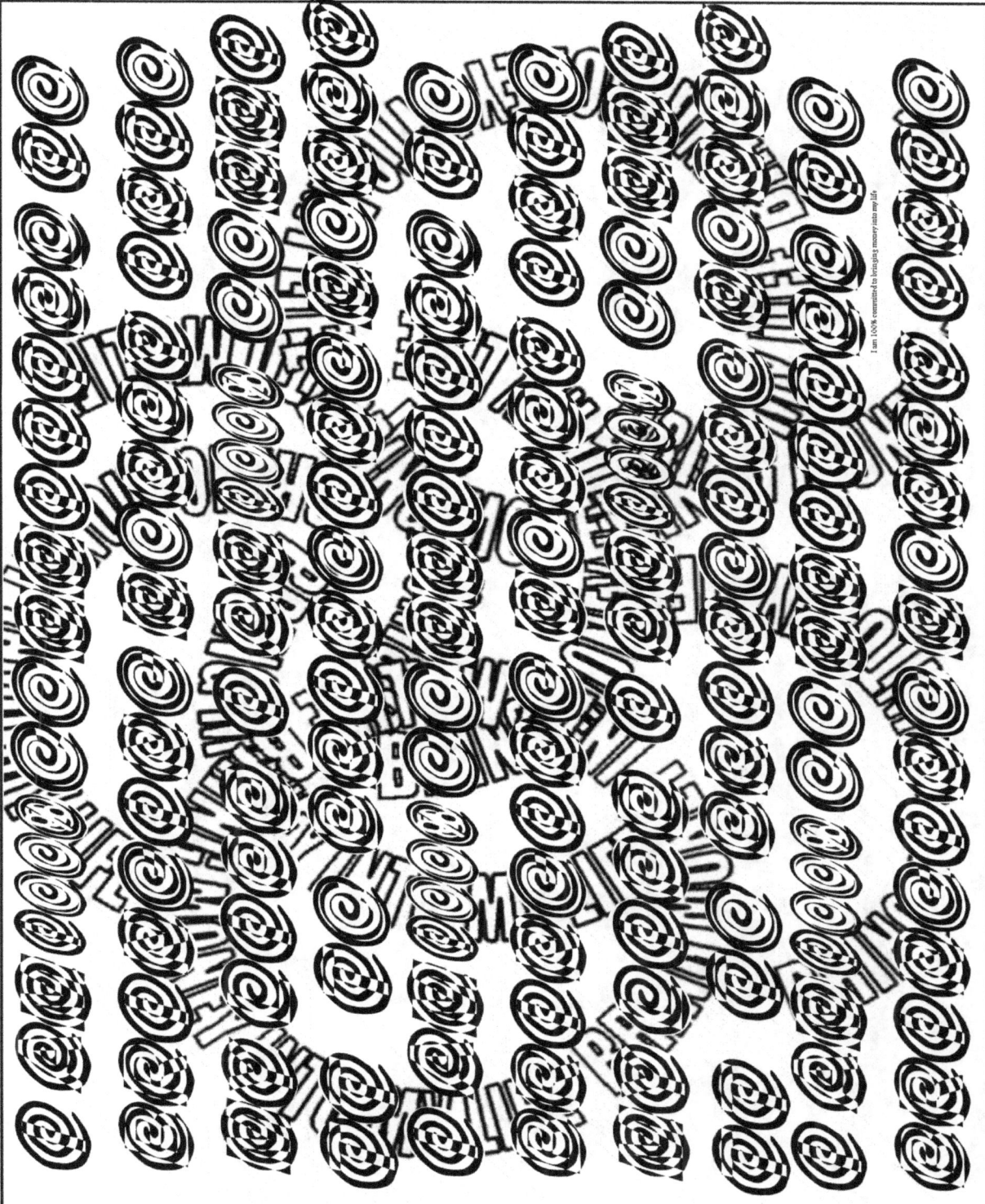

I am 100% committed to bringing money into my life

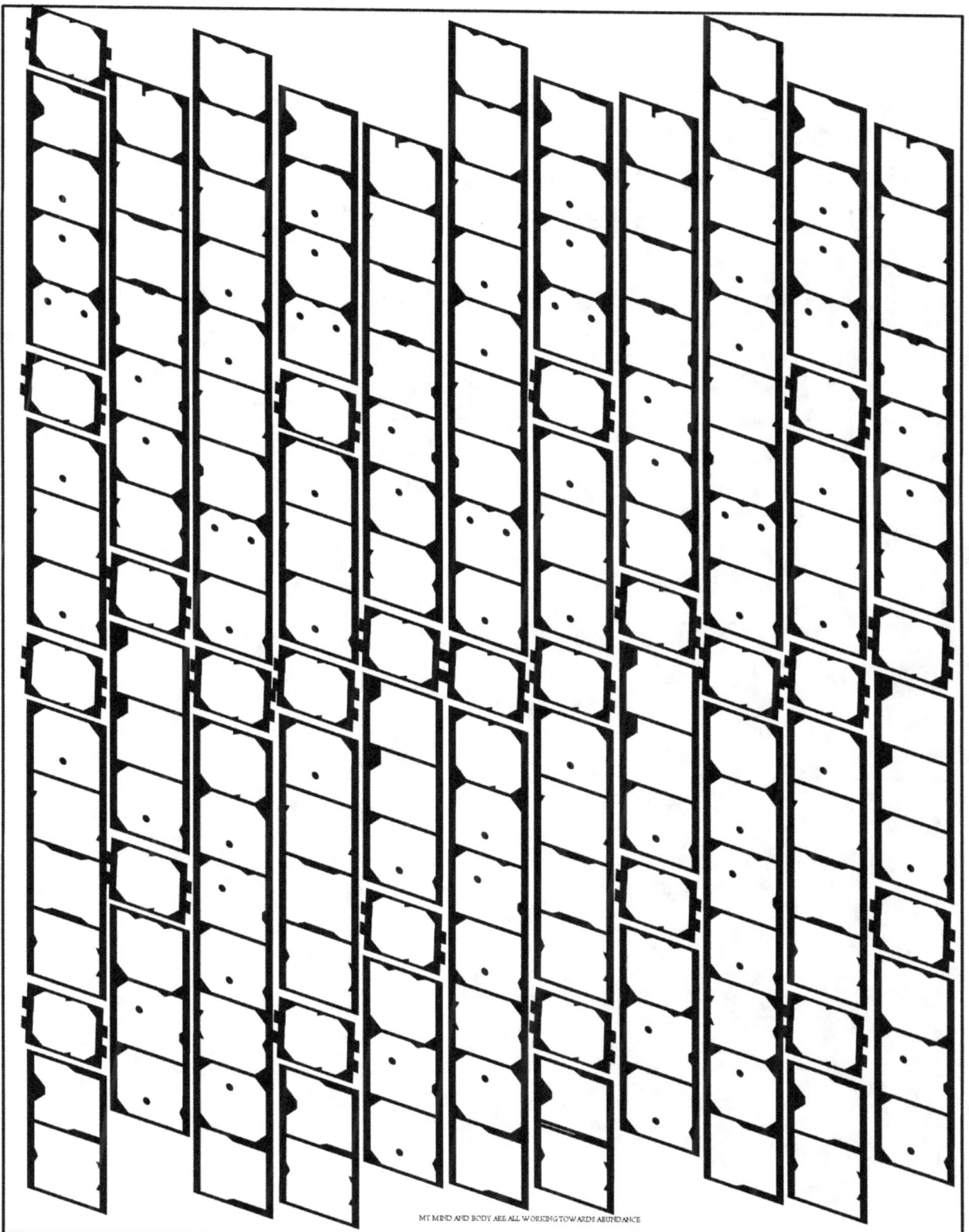

MY MIND AND BODY ARE ALL WORKING TOWARDS ABUNDANCE

I AM ACHEIVING MY FINANCIAL FREEDOM NOW I A
ACHEIVING MY FINANCIAL FREEDOM NOW I AM ACH
MY FINANCIAL FREEDOM NOW I AM ACHEIVING MY
FINANCIAL FREEDOM NOW I AM ACHEIVING MY FIN
FREEDOM NOW I AM ACHEIVING MY FINANCIAL FRE
NOW I AM ACHEIVING MY FINANCIAL FREEDOM NOW
I AM ACHEIVING MY FINANCIAL FREEDOM NOW I A
ACHEIVING MY FINANCIAL FREEDOM NOW I AM ACH
MY FINANCIAL FREEDOM NOW I AM ACHEIVING MY
FINANCIAL FREEDOM NOW I AM ACHEIVING MY FIN

I AM ACHEIVING MY FINANCIAL FREEDOM NOW

FREEDOM NOW I AM ACHEIVING MY FINANCIAL FRE
NOW I AM ACHEIVING MY FINANCIAL FREEDOM NOW

I am passionate about building wealth. I am passionate about building wealth. I am passionate about building wealth. I am passionate about building wealth. I am passionate about building wealth. I am passionate about building wealth. I am passionate about building wealth. I am passionate about building wealth. I am passionate about building wealth. I am passionate about building wealth. I am passionate about building wealth. I am passionate about building wealth. I am so passionate about building wealth. I am passionate about building wealth. I am passionate about building wealth.

I deserve to have

financial abundance

in my life. Yes Sir, I

do deserve to have

more money and

financial abundance

in my life. More money.

I deserve to have financial abundance in my life

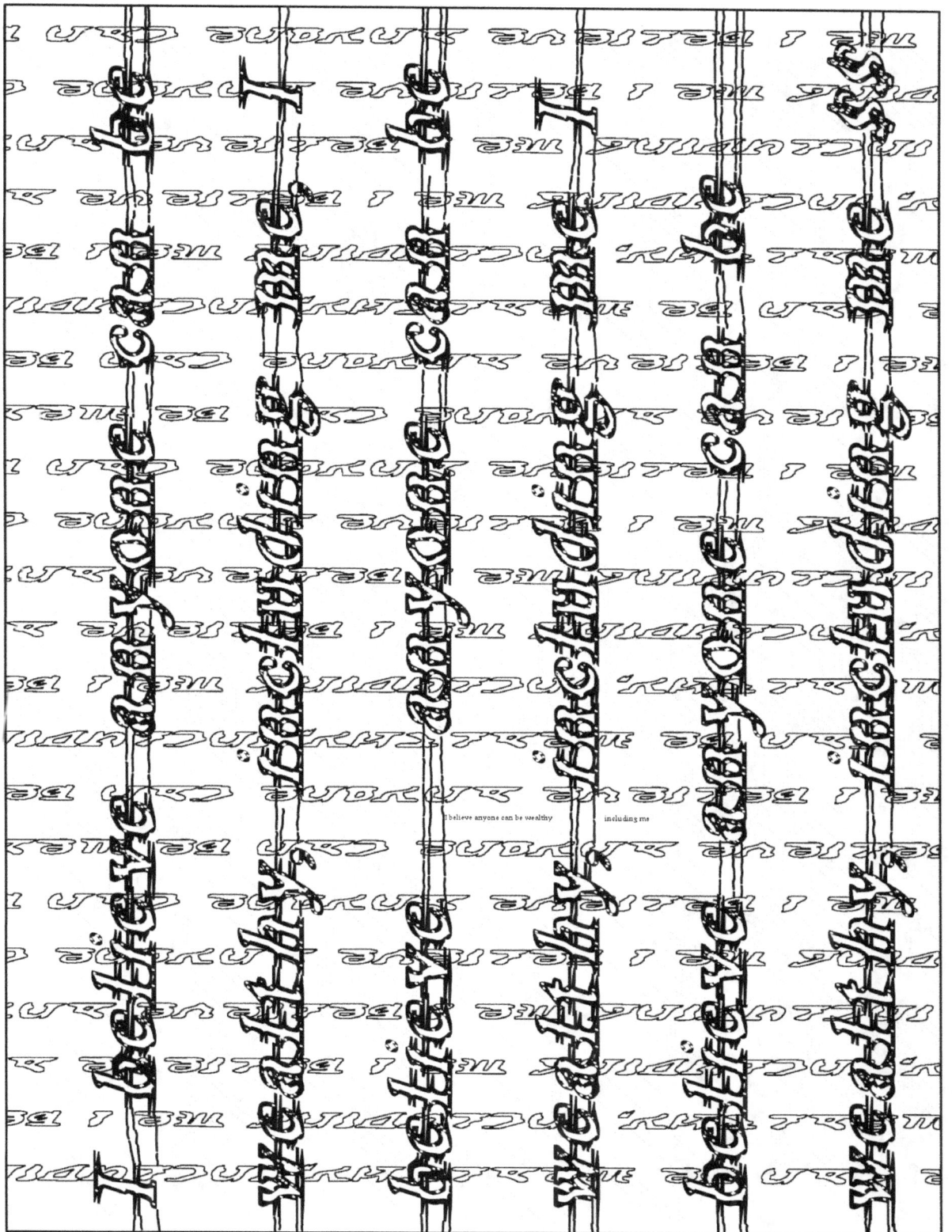

I believe anyone can be wealthy   including me

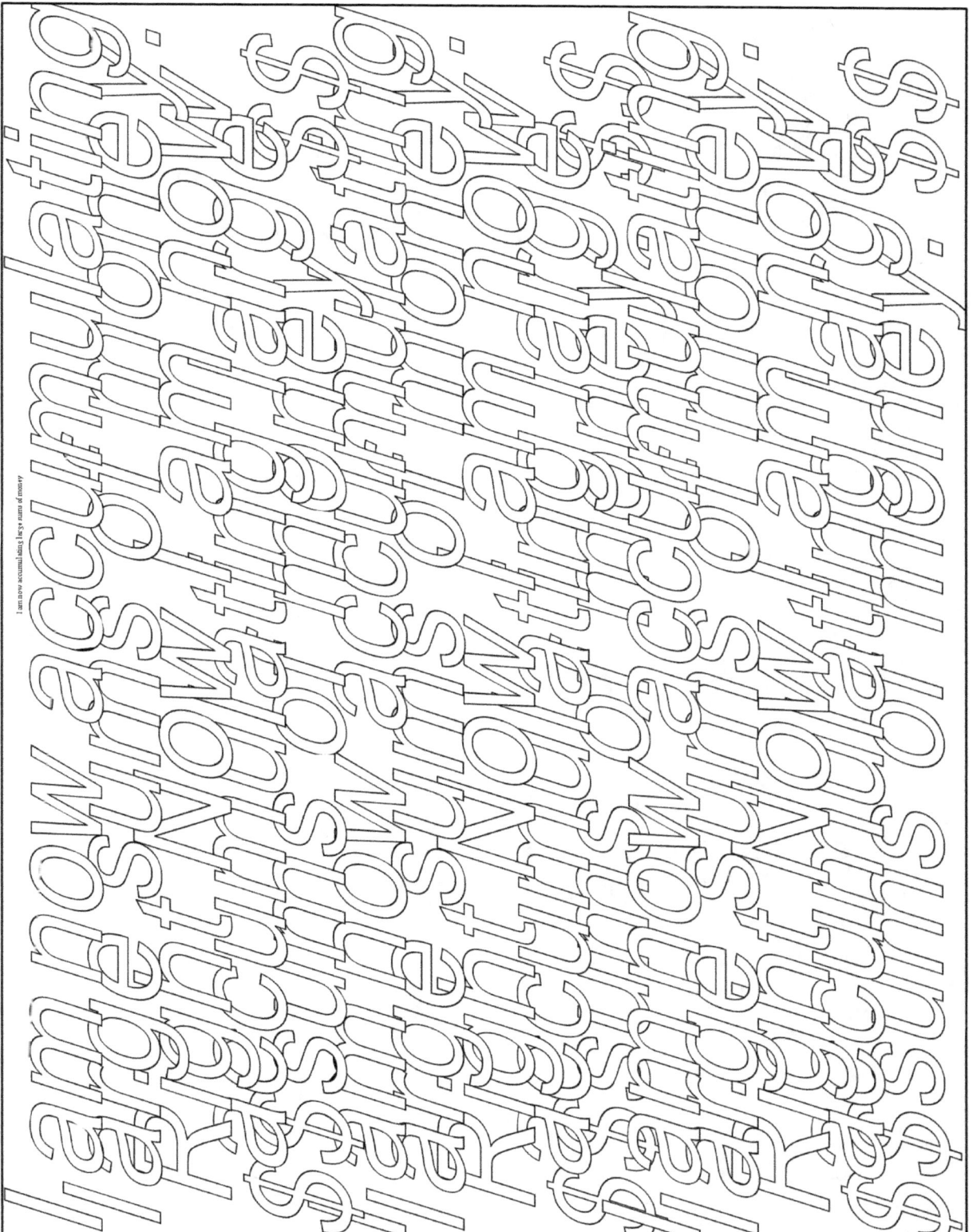

I am now accumulating sums of money that I am now accumulating.

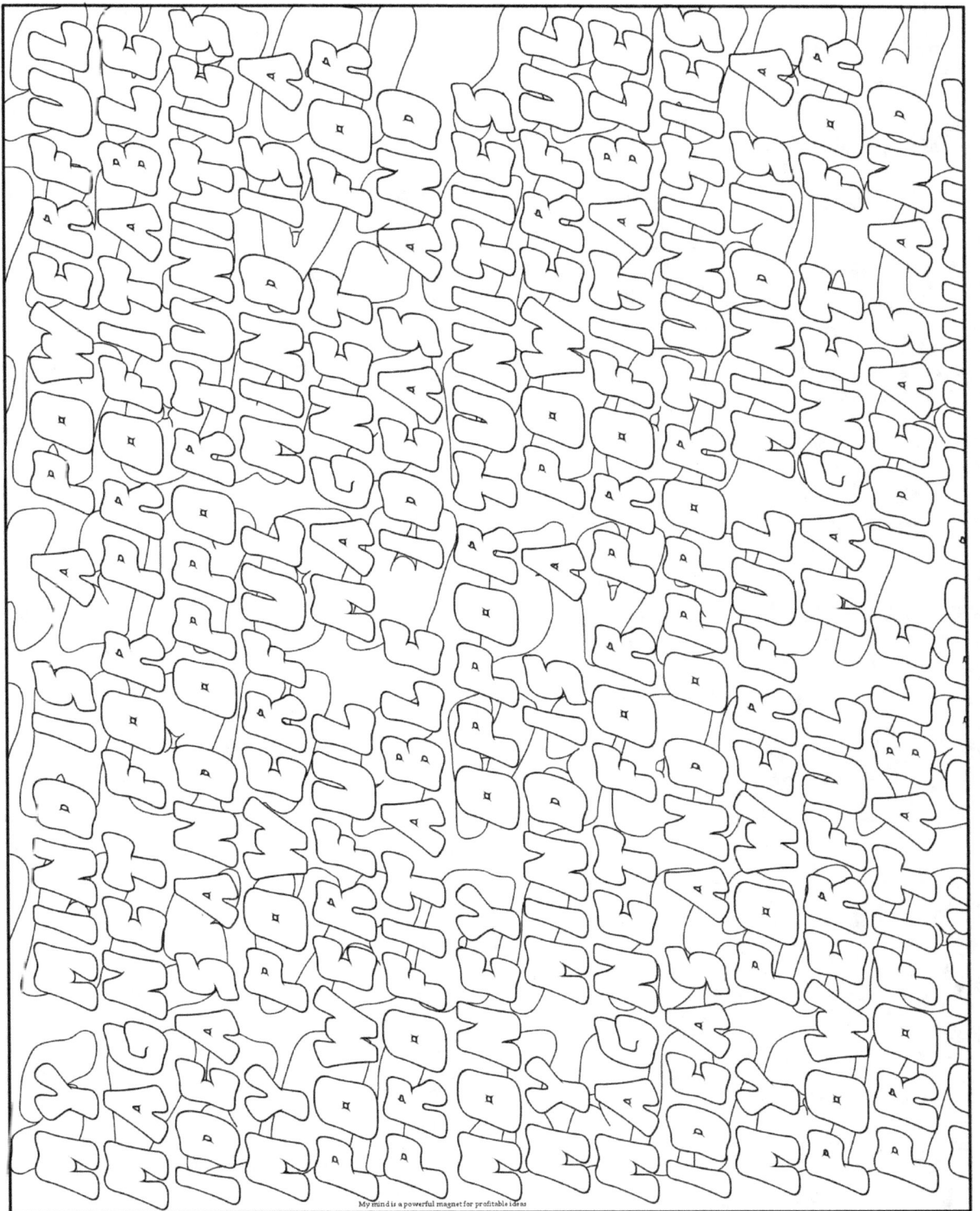

My mind is a powerful magnet for profitable ideas

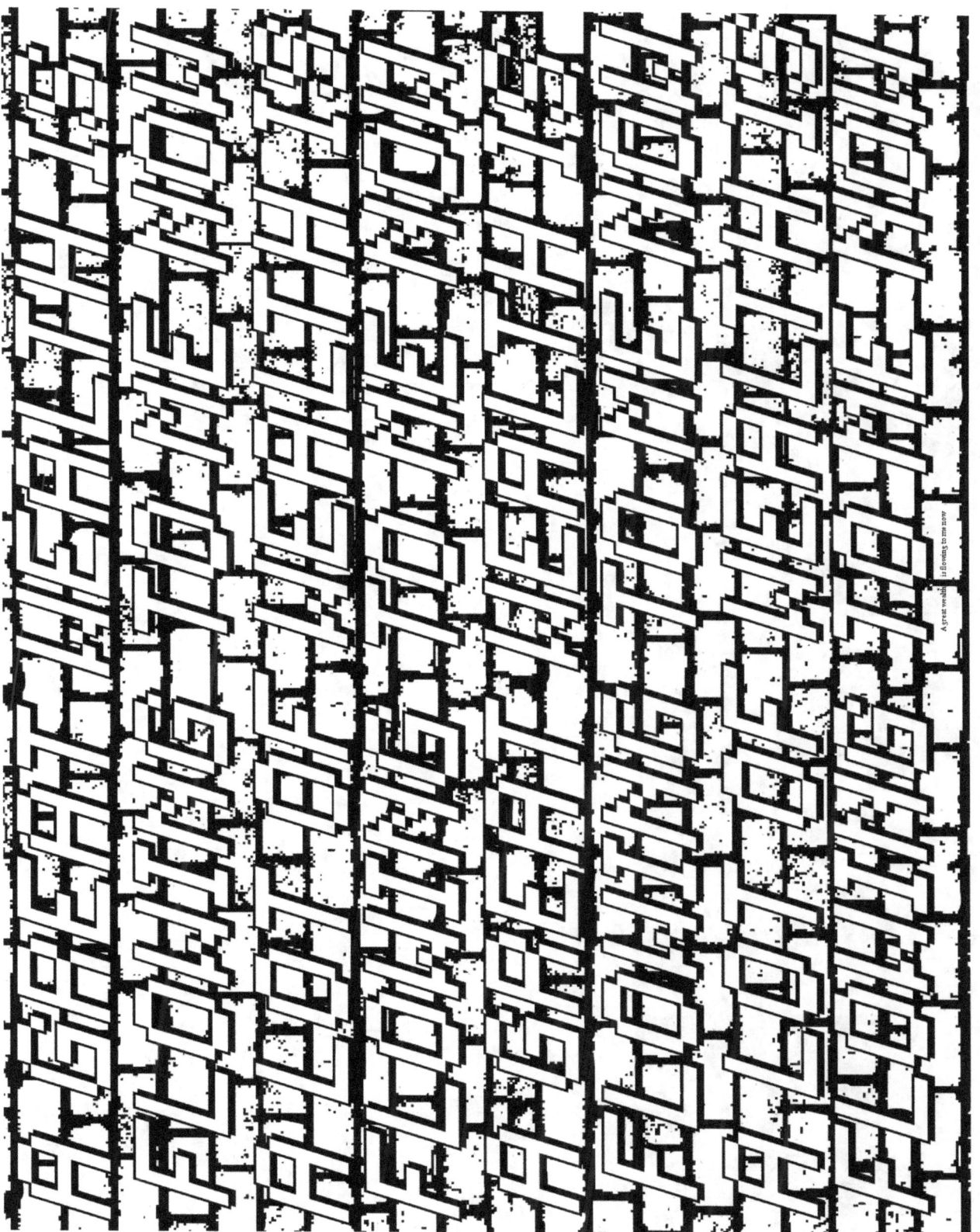

A great wealth is flowing to me now

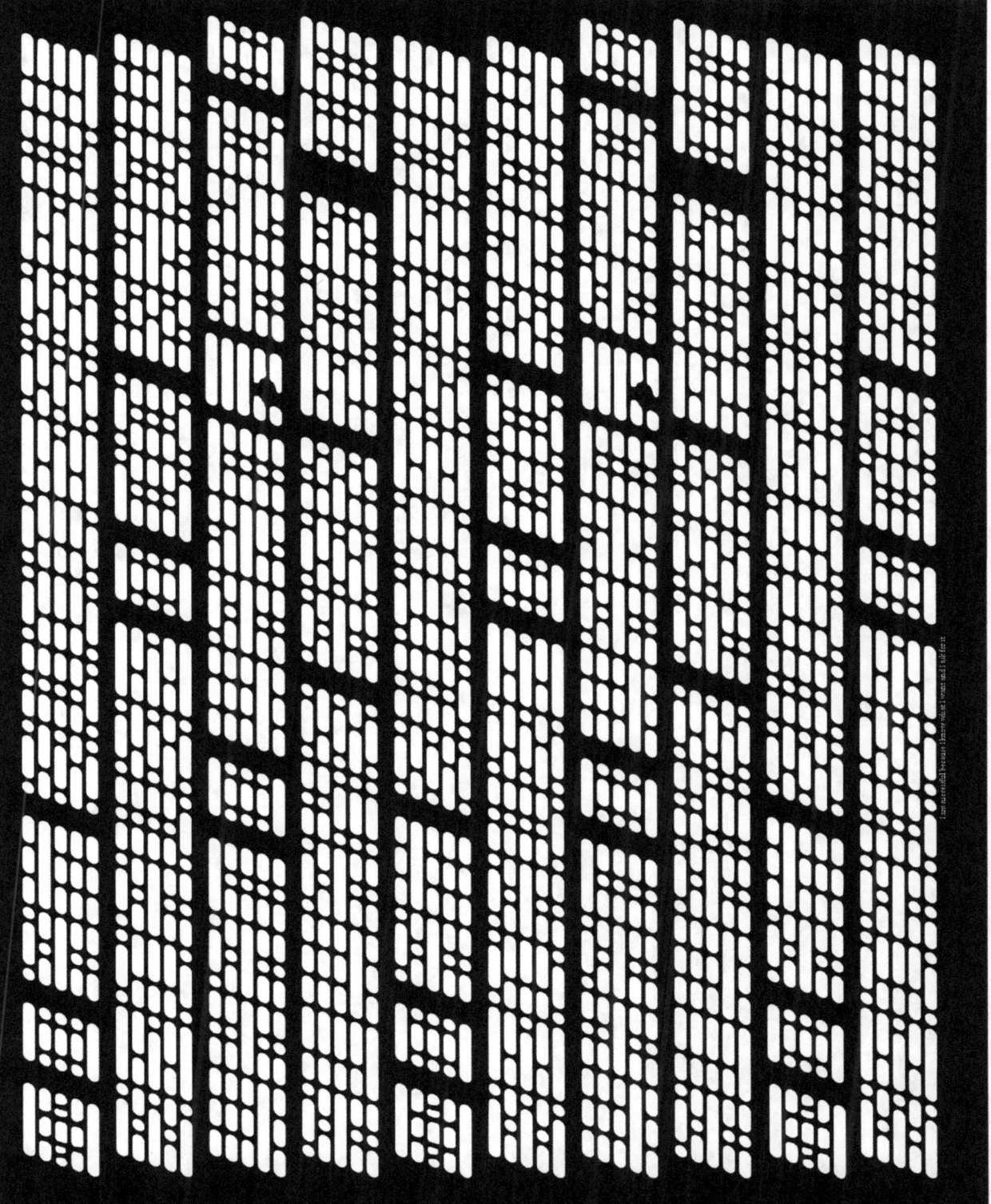

I create wealth easily and effortlessly

I define success my way

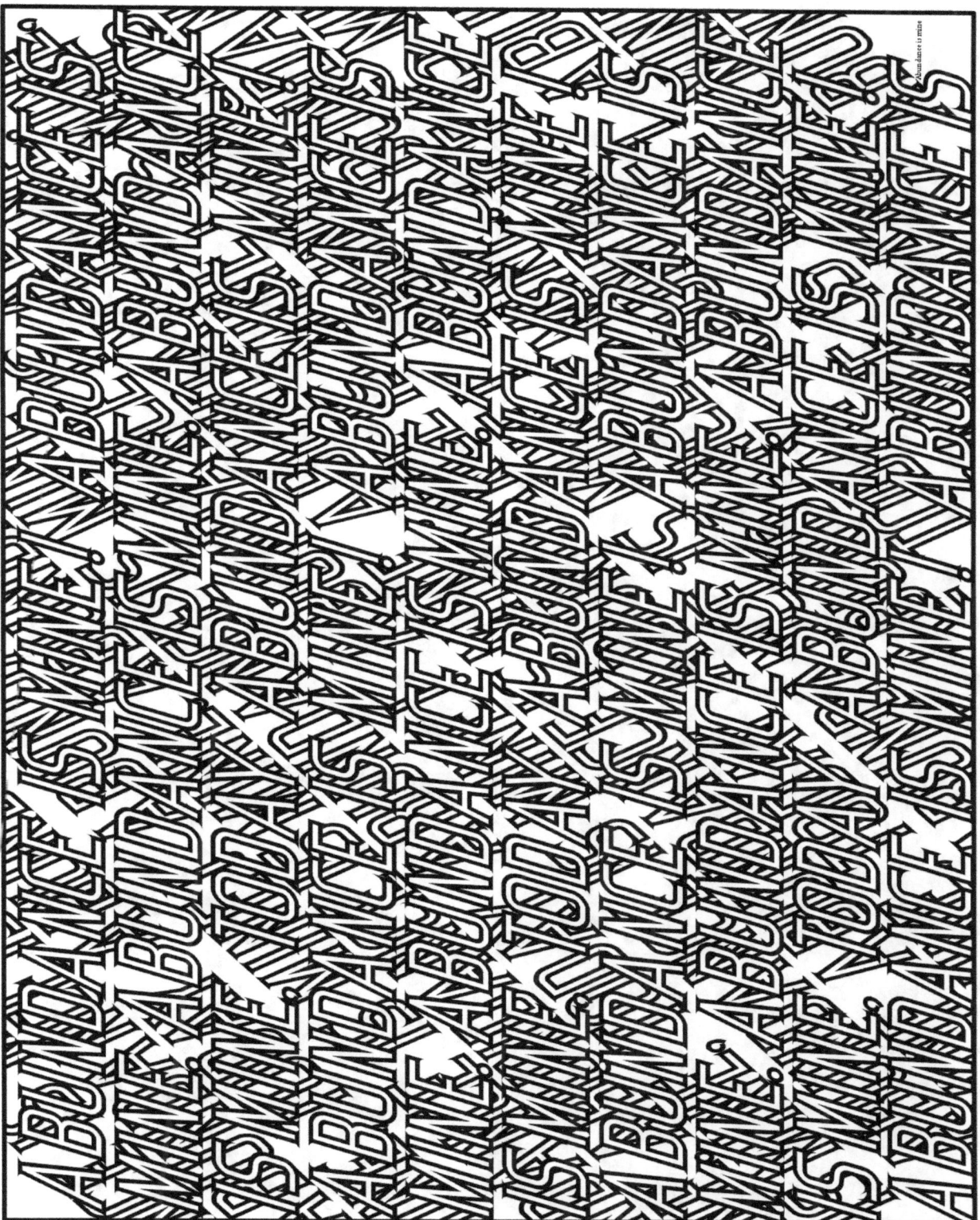

Right now i am gaining wealth

Right now i am gaining wealth

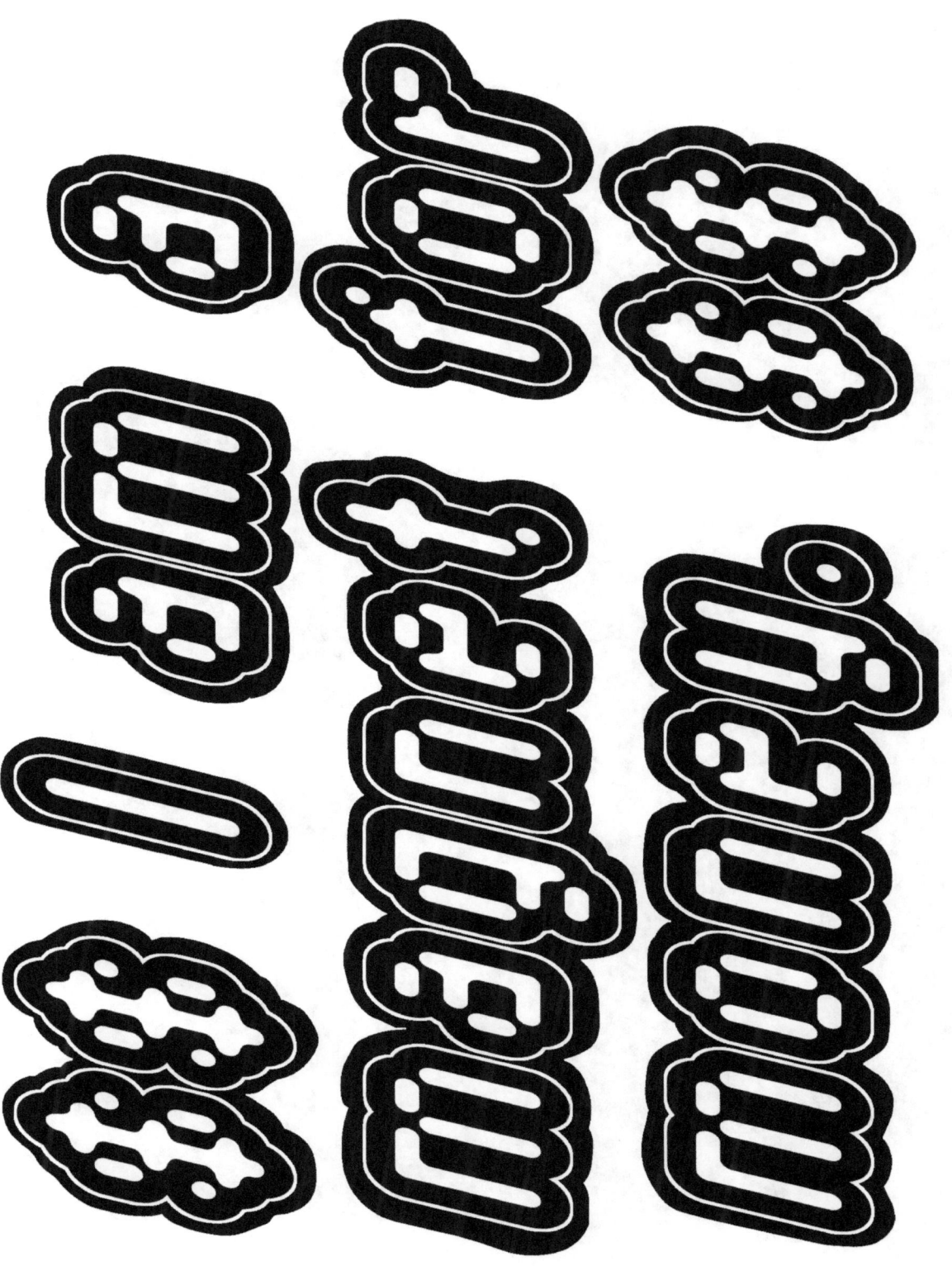

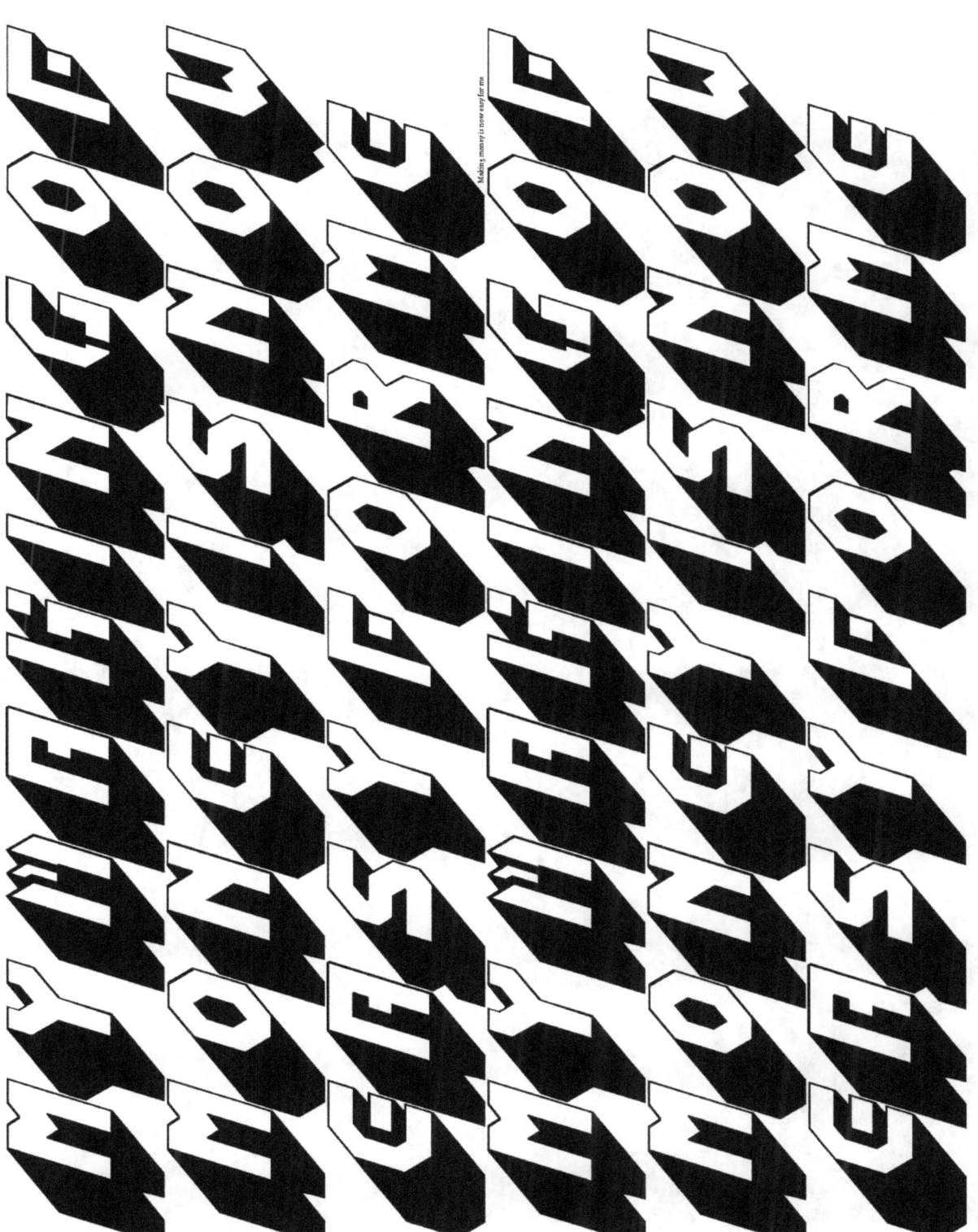

Making money is now easy for me

You can order large poster sized coloring pages of my designs from my website at Etsy.com Not only do I supply large sized images of the pages in this book, but images of Hawaiian scenes and even the Trump family from my other books. Make colorful posters for your room!

I have over a hundred large Hawaiian canvas prints and paintings, and nearly 200 smaller watercolor/prints at my Etsy art site. The coloring book pages of my Hawaiian Scene coloring books are based on some of these paintings. If you like my Hawaiian art, check all of these out at hawaiiseascapes.etsy.com

Check out my other books at Amazon. I have these books currently published:

Romantic and Fairy Tale Vintage Illustrations an Adult Coloring Book
Old time ink and woodcut illustrations.

The Making of Romantic and Fairy Tale Vintage Illustrations, an Illustrated Book for Adults The description and illustration of each page above.

 The Making of Psychedelic Brain Freeze: An Illustrated Book for Adults
(explains the science behind optical illusions, shows how to color large poster sized pages to make your own art.)

The Making of Psychedelic Brain Freeze II: An Illustrated Book for Adults
(explains the science for more optical illusions, shows how to color large poster sized pages to make your own wall art.)

 Relaxing Hawaiian Scenes, An Adult Coloring Book   (first in the series)

Relaxing Hawaiian Scenes II, An Adult Coloring Book (2nd in the series)

The Making of Relaxing Hawaiian Scenes II, An Adult Illustrated Book

Relaxing Hawaiian Scenes III, An Adult Coloring Book　(3rd in the series)

The Making of Relaxing Hawaiian Scenes III, An Adult Illustrated Book

Portraits of President Donald Trump and the First Family: an Adult Coloring Book (attractive personal pictures of all of President Trump's family)

Making of Portraits of President Donald Trump and the First Family, An Illustrated Book (explains some of the hidden Easter egg images in the drawings)

How to Import From China Starting With $250 and Make a Small Fortune!

Creation of the Universe and Other Strange Mormon Beliefs Revealed. (A church member tells all the Secrets the Authorities Don't Want to Talk About.)

How To Use Your Money Making Genes to Become a Success and Make a Small Fortune.

How to Publish Books on Amazon Kindle and Make a Small Fortune, The E-Book Money Making System

Thanks....